MOON
LANDING

THE RACE FOR THE
MOON

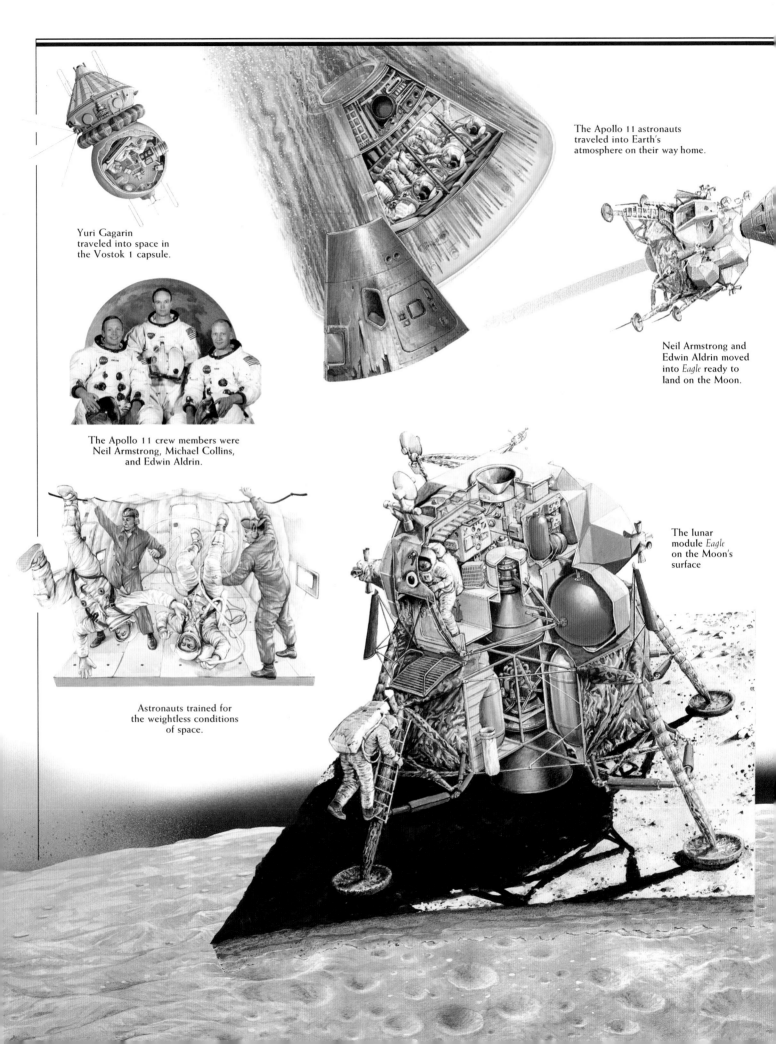

Yuri Gagarin traveled into space in the Vostok 1 capsule.

The Apollo 11 astronauts traveled into Earth's atmosphere on their way home.

Neil Armstrong and Edwin Aldrin moved into *Eagle* ready to land on the Moon.

The Apollo 11 crew members were Neil Armstrong, Michael Collins, and Edwin Aldrin.

The lunar module *Eagle* on the Moon's surface

Astronauts trained for the weightless conditions of space.

MOON
LANDING
THE RACE FOR THE MOON

Written by
CAROLE STOTT
Illustrated by
RICHARD BONSON

A DK PUBLISHING BOOK
www.dk.com

A DK Publishing Book
www.dk.com

Senior Editor Scarlett O'Hara
Senior Art Editor Vicky Wharton
Senior Managing Editor Linda Martin
Senior Managing Art Editor Julia Harris
DTP Designer Andrew O'Brien
Picture Research Amanda Russell
Jacket Designer Andrew Nash
Production Kate Oliver
US Editors Constance Robinson and Lilan Patri

First American edition, 1999

2 4 6 8 10 9 7 5 3

Published in the United States by DK Publishing, Inc.
95 Madison Avenue, New York, New York 10016

Published in Great Britain by Dorling Kindersley Ltd.

Library of Congress Cataloging-in-Publication Data

Stott, Carole.
    Moon landing / by Carole Stott. --1st American ed.
        p.   cm. -- (DK discoveries)
    Summary: An illustrated account of humanity's exploration of
the moon, from our first observations and attempts to the first
landing and later expeditions.
    ISBN 0-7894-3958-1
    1. Space flight to the moon--Juvenile literature.
2. Astronautics--History--Juvenile literature. [1. Space flight to
the Moon.] I. Title. II. Series.
TL799.M6S83 1999
629.45′4--dc21   99-11937
                                                                      CIP

Reproduced by Colourscan, Singapore
Printed and bound by L.E.G.O., Italy

Additional illustrations by Andrew Wheatcroft and
David Ashby

Contents

Looking into Space

FOR THOUSANDS OF YEARS, PEOPLE ON Earth have looked into space and seen the Moon. Its bright, full disk lit up the dark night hours for early people, and inspired countless myths and stories. Its changing face and movement across the sky marked the passage of time. The Moon has always been a fascinating place that some people dreamed of visiting. About a hundred years ago, these dreams started to come true.

Dark areas indicate lower, flatter regions where a spacecraft could land.

Large bowl-shaped hollows, called craters, can be seen from Earth.

THE FIRST MAN IN SPACE

Yuri Gagarin
Gagarin was 27 when he made his historic flight into space. He trained to be a metal worker but had learned to fly in his spare time so that he could join the Soviet Air Force. He became a test pilot, flying new and experimental aircraft. In 1960, Yuri joined a small team of cosmonauts (Soviet astronauts) training for space. Less than a year later, he was chosen to make the first manned flight.

IN EARLY 1961, SPACE SCIENTISTS IN the US and the USSR were working towards launching a human into space. Many people believed that the first flight might be just weeks, or at the most, months away. But when, on April 12, 1961, television stations and newspapers proclaimed, "Gagarin: First Man in Space," almost everyone was taken by surprise. There had been no launch party or live television coverage of the event, and few people knew that there was to be a flight that day. Now Yuri Gagarin was a hero, and his achievement was talked about around the world.

The retro-rocket fired to prepare for reentry to Earth's atmosphere.

The instrument module housed equipment for guiding and controlling the craft in orbit, as well as its braking systems.

Gagarin's flight lasted one orbit of Earth, giving him plenty of time to experience weightlessness.

During his flight, Gagarin constantly answered questions and carried out assignments.

Vostok's orbit

Engels

Baikonur Cosmodrome

Caspian Sea

Aral Sea

Gagarin's rocket

GAGARIN'S ROCKET was a Vostok A1. It launched him into space in three stages and had completed its work within minutes.

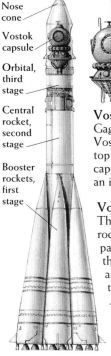

Nose cone

Vostok capsule

Orbital, third stage

Central rocket, second stage

Booster rockets, first stage

Gagarin's round cabin

Instrument module

Vostok 1 capsule
Gagarin traveled in the Vostok 1 capsule at the top of the rocket. The capsule had a cabin and an instrument module.

Vostok A1 launcher
The first stage lifted the rocket off the launch pad, the second boosted the craft into space, and the third placed the spacecraft in orbit. All three stages and the nose cone were discarded once their work was finished.

THE BEGINNING
The Vostok A1 rocket started its journey into space at 9:07 a.m. Moscow time, on April 12, 1961. It set off from the Baikonur Cosmodrome, east of the Aral Sea in the Soviet Union. Gagarin's wife Valya saw him off.

TAKEOFF
Gagarin heard a roar, and the rocket quivered as it left the launch pad. As he moved away from the ground, gravity pulled him down into his seat.

IN ORBIT
Vostok 1 traveled at about 17,400 mph (28,000 kph) and orbited Earth at between 112 and 203 miles (181 and 327 km) above the ground.

SAFE LANDING

The dangerous part of the flight for Gagarin was the return to Earth. As he passed over Africa, the retro-rockets fired, and Vostok 1 slowed down and came out of orbit. Gagarin's craft would land automatically, but he was ready to pilot it himself if necessary. As he left space, gravity pushed him into his seat, and he prepared to be ejected.

The instrument module separated from the cabin before the return to Earth.

ALL GOING WELL
Gagarin sucked water from a tube and found that drops floated around the cabin. The flight had no ill effects on Gagarin. Both his heartbeat and breathing were normal.

The complete capsule was 7.9 ft (2.4 m) in diameter.

Gagarin's small parachute opened first.

4.3 miles (7 km) above the ground the capsule hatch blew off and Gagarin was ejected in his seat.

At 2.5 miles (4 km) above the ground the main parachute opened, and the ejector seat fell to Earth.

Gagarin and Vostok 1 landed in fields 16 miles (26 km) southwest of Engels.

A camera in the cabin recorded Gagarin's movements.

ON THE GROUND
Gagarin returned to Earth by a separate parachute from Vostok 1. His main parachute slowed his fall so that he moved at about 16 ft (5 m) per second when he reached the ground.

Returning to Earth
The capsule showed the scars of its return from space. As it traveled through the atmosphere, the outside of the capsule became intensely hot. Gagarin noticed a red glow outside, but inside the temperature didn't rise. The capsule's heat-resistant cover successfully protected him.

CRASH LANDING
The capsule returned to Earth by parachute. This landing would have been too harsh for an astronaut inside.

The return to Earth was at 10:55 a.m. Moscow time, 108 minutes after launch.

COSMONAUT TRAINER
Gagarin became the head of cosmonaut training, but he never returned to space. He was killed test-flying a plane in 1968.

During the flight, Gagarin recorded his experiences with a pencil in a log book; when he let them go, they floated in the weightlessness of space.

AROUND THE WORLD

Gagarin's space journey took him once around the earth. He traveled eastward, moving over his own country from the launch site, then over South America and Africa. From launch to landing, the journey lasted 108 minutes. While in flight, he achieved many firsts: as well as being the first person in space, he was also the first person to talk to Earth from space and the first person to eat in space.

> ❝ **"Weightlessness does not feel unpleasant. Am feeling fine. All instruments and all systems are functioning well."** ❞
>
> **Yuri Gagarin during his spaceflight, April 12, 1961**

A world hero
Everyone wanted to meet the man who had been into space. Gagarin visited countries around the world, including England (above). Wherever he went crowds gathered. He was met by world leaders, given honors and medals, and his hometown of Gzhatsk was renamed Gagarin.

Target: the Moon

THE FIRST MAN IN SPACE, YURI GAGARIN, BLASTED OFF in April 1961. Other astronauts got their chance in the months and years to come. The space travelers came from the Soviet Union and the United States. At first they went singly, then in crews of two or three. They stayed in the space close to Earth. But longer missions were being planned. Future trips would take humans to another world – the Moon.

In 1965, Ed White became the first American astronaut to leave his craft and walk in space.

White's suit supplied oxygen to breathe.

A tether secured White to the Gemini 4 capsule.

THE SPACE RACE

GAGARIN'S SUCCESSFUL SPACE FLIGHT IN April 1961 surprised the US. They reacted by declaring that they would send a man to the Moon by the end of the 1960s. Perhaps the Soviets were also aiming to land a man on the Moon. No one was sure. But the two nations began an unofficial race. They both wanted to be the first to make significant steps in space travel. The Soviets launched the first woman into space, took the first space walk, and landed the first craft on the Moon. The Americans flew the Mercury and Gemini missions putting crews of two and then three men in space, they achieved the first meeting of two craft in space, and made the first space docking. The US slowly gained the lead in the space race and moved closer to its goal.

A DAY IN SPACE

Cosmonaut Gherman Titov was the second Soviet in space. His flight aboard Vostok 2 in August 1961 was four months after Yuri Gagarin's. Titov was the first to spend more than a day in space; his flight lasted more than 25 hours.

AMERICAN HERO

John Glenn (left) was the first American to orbit Earth. His Mercury 6 capsule, named *Friendship 7*, carried him around Earth three times on February 20, 1962. Back home he was greeted by President John F. Kennedy.

THE MERCURY 7

The first astronauts from the US traveled into space in bell-shaped capsules, only 9 ft (2.7 m) long. The seven astronauts, chosen in 1959, were known as the Mercury 7. All flights made by the astronauts, between July 1961 and May 1963, were successful. America's second space program called Gemini began in 1964. Gemini missions carried two men and stayed in space longer.

Alan Shepard

Virgil Grissom

Gordon Cooper

Donald Slayton

John Glenn

Walter Schirra

Scott Carpenter

FIRST WOMAN

Soviet cosmonaut Valentina Tereshkova was the first woman to go into space. She was chosen from a group of five women who trained for the flight. Her capsule Vostok 6 orbited the Earth for three days in June 1963. Her flight took her within 3 miles (4.8 km) of another cosmonaut who spent five days inside Vostok 5.

Leonov tumbled around in space for 12 minutes.

A camera was attached to the edge of the air lock.

Leonov moved from the capsule through an air lock into space.

A porthole with a sighting device

Pavel Belyayev, Leonov's fellow cosmonaut, remained inside Voskhod 2.

Nitrogen and oxygen fuel tanks

A communication antenna unfolded once the capsule was in space.

SPACE WALK

The first astronaut to go outside a craft in space was the Soviet cosmonaut Alexei Leonov in March 1965. His extra vehicular activity (EVA), more usually called a space walk, lasted a little longer than expected. His suit had expanded when he was outside the craft, and it was a tight squeeze to get back in through the hatch.

This photograph was taken by the astronauts on board Gemini 6 as they approached Gemini 7 in space.

SPACE RENDEZVOUS

Gemini craft achieved the first rendezvous, or meeting, in space in December 1965. It was an essential maneuver for a mission to the Moon. Gemini 7 was already in space when Gemini 6 was launched. To achieve the rendezvous, Gemini 6 flew within 2 ft (60 cm) of Gemini 7.

Circular rendezvous-antenna in the nose

Gemini 7

Luna 3 took the first photographs of the far side of the Moon.

DOCKING IN SPACE

The next stage after attaining a space rendezvous was for two craft to dock (to meet and then join together) in space. The US gained another space first when Gemini 8 docked with an uncrewed Agena rocket (above) in March 1966. Gemini 8 was guided by astronaut Neil Armstrong.

The Luna program
A series of space probes called Luna accomplished many "firsts" for the Soviets. Luna 3 was the first craft to travel around the Moon. Luna 9, in February 1966, made the first controlled landing and sent back the first pictures from the lunar surface. Its success proved the lunar surface could support a spacecraft. In the same year, Luna 10 became the first craft to orbit the Moon.

Luna 3

ASTRONAUT TRAINING AND SELECTION

THE US SERIES OF MISSIONS TO CARRY humans to the Moon was called Apollo. The astronauts chosen for the missions underwent months of training to prepare them for their journey. They prepared for the challenges of space, and trained for the work they had to do on each part of their journey. Hours were spent in mock-up spacecraft learning flying and landing procedures. They practiced tasks such as eating in space, as well as emergency routines. They prepared their bodies for the different forces they would feel, from the increased gravity at launch, to the weightlessness of space, and the reduced gravity on the Moon's surface.

Weightlessness

A SPECIAL AIRCRAFT following a flight path called a parabolic loop can produce weightless conditions.

KC-135 plane at the top of its loop

23,000 ft

19,700 ft

17,200 ft

Reduced gravity
As the plane flies on the downward part of its path, anyone inside feels weightless for about 25 seconds. Though gravity is still there, passengers cannot feel it because they are falling around the Earth.

FEELING WEIGHTLESS
Weightlessness can be achieved for only a short period of time during the flight of a specially adapted aircraft. Astronauts in their space suits made about 40 flights to practice moving while weightless.

The plane is padded to prevent injury.

Technicians secure themselves so that they can help the astronauts.

When the astronauts are weightless, they "fly" around inside the craft.

Astronauts appear to be upside down, but there is no up or down in the weightlessness of space.

To move forward, an astronaut needs to move backward in space.

MOON WALKING
Astronauts prepared for getting around on the Moon by walking while they were supported by a sling and wires. The apparatus held an astronaut's body parallel to the ground and took 5/6ths of his weight to simulate the Moon's gravity.

UNDERWATER TRAINING
A giant water tank containing a mock-up of the lunar module helped astronauts prepare for the weaker gravitational pull on the Moon. They wore weights on their suits to give them buoyancy and practiced getting into and out of the mock-up of the lunar module.

Increased gravity

WHEN ASTRONAUTS accelerate away from Earth and then decelerate on return to Earth, they feel increased gravity. The first experience is within seconds of liftoff. For a short time, the force felt is 3G, three times the usual pull of gravity.

Spinning around
A centrifuge machine helps to prepare astronauts for the increased forces they will feel when they travel into space. The astronaut (on the left above) is strapped into a seat and spun around and around to experience forces up to 8G.

Testing the human body
Before any human had flown into space, tests were carried out to see if the human body could cope with increased gravity. Once it was proved that it could, astronauts prepared for the greater gravitational forces of space flight.

A harness secured his body.

The head and facial features are pushed back.

The deceleration force is 22G.

1 In 1954, to test responses to sudden changes in force, Lieutenant Colonel John Stapp was sent hurtling down a track at Holloman Air Force Base, New Mexico.

2 Stapp roared down the track for five seconds, reaching speeds of over 600 mph (970 kph). The effect of the force of 12G can be seen on his face.

3 The seat jolted to a stop. Stapp's head lurched forward, he was blinded for a few seconds, and gained black eyes when blood surged to his face.

MAKING A LANDING
A vehicle nicknamed the "flying bedstead" was used to train for landing the lunar module. The craft would be flown by the commander of a mission. On one occasion, when Neil Armstrong was flying the bedstead, it began to tilt. He ejected safely before it crashed to the ground.

SAFE EXIT
In an emergency, an astronaut can eject from the training vehicle. He is catapulted high into the air and floats down by parachute.

The Lunar Landing Training Vehicle

Thrusters alter the position of the bedstead to prepare it for a smooth landing.

A computer on board eliminates 5/6ths of gravity to simulate lunar conditions.

KEEPING COOL
The astronauts practiced wearing their space suits and moving around on rough terrain. One important job of the suit was to keep the wearer's temperature constant. The astronaut on the right is wearing water-cooled underwear under his suit. On the left, the material of an oversuit is tested.

FACT file

• The first American astronauts were recruited in 1959. They were all male, under 40 years of age, and qualified jet pilots with 1,500 hours of flying experience.

• The typical Apollo astronaut was 5 ft 10 in (1.8 m) tall, weighed 160 lb (72.5 kg), and was 38.6 years old when he first flew in space.

• Of the 29 Apollo astronauts, seven were left-handed and 22 were the first-born in their family, and 27 were married.

Neil Armstrong   Michael Collins   Edwin Aldrin

The Apollo 11 crew
There were 29 astronauts who trained for the Apollo missions to the Moon. No one knew who would be the crew of three chosen to make the first landing. All the astronauts were capable of making that special flight. The crew was announced in January 1969. Neil Armstrong was to be the commander, and he would be accompanied to the lunar surface by Edwin "Buzz" Aldrin. Michael Collins would stay in orbit around the Moon.

PREPARING FOR THE MOON

ALL OVER THE US, PEOPLE WERE WORKING toward the first manned landing on the Moon. From 1961 onward, thousands of workers, each concerned with a small part of the mission, prepared their contributions. As the astronauts trained and engineers designed and built the spacecraft, other teams prepared food, made clothes, devised tools for rock-collecting, and tested cameras to record the first steps on another world. Robotic craft were sent to photograph the lunar surface and find the right place for a lunar landing. Probes touched down to examine the surface on which astronauts would walk. Then the various parts of the complex journey were tried out by Apollo astronauts.

ON CAMERA
There were six television cameras inside the Ranger. They operated from when it first approached the Moon until it crash-landed on the surface.

Solar panels on either side provided the power for the cameras and for transmitting the pictures to Earth.

PHOTOGRAPHING THE MOON
A series of nine space probes called Ranger were designed to provide the first close-up views of the lunar surface. Only the final three in the series, launched between 1964 and 1965, were successful. They sent back more than 17,000 photographs showing detail that was invisible to telescopes on Earth.

Pineapple juice   Sugar cookies

Space food
The food for the Apollo astronauts had to be nutritious, ready to eat, easy to consume in weightless conditions, and neither bulky nor heavy. Some of the food was dehydrated; some was kept moist. Most food was in sealed pouches; the drink pouches had a nozzle for sucking out the contents. The astronauts chose a menu for space from the 75 drinks and 100 food items available.

A camera with two lenses took photographs of the lunar surface.

RECORDED IMAGES
The information from the camera was recorded and radioed to Earth, where images were built up in strips.

CLOSE-UP VIEW
Lunar Orbiter 2 was 28.4 miles (45.7 km) above the Moon's surface when it recorded this view on November 28, 1966. Orbiter's photographs showed the mountains and plains of the lunar landscape.

CHOOSING A LANDING SITE
Almost the entire surface of the Moon was mapped by five Lunar Orbiter space probes starting in August 1966. The craft also provided images of selected areas that were then used to choose a landing site for the crewed missions. Orbiter developed its photographs on board and relayed the results back to Earth.

MAKING A LANDING

Seven Surveyor craft traveled to the Moon between June 1966 and January 1968. Their purpose was to make a soft-landing on the Moon using a retro-engine to slow their descent. On board were scientific instruments that tested the surface and a scoop that dug into the soil.

TESTING THE SURFACE
Surveyor photographed its own footpad on the surface of the Moon, showing that a craft would not sink into the lunar soil.

A solar-powered television camera took pictures of the landscape in all directions.

Surveyor had shock-absorbing footpads to help it to soft-land on the surface.

PRACTICING FOR THE MOON

Two Apollo missions carried men to the Moon before Apollo 11. The first crewed trip was made by Apollo 8, which orbited the Moon ten times. Apollo 10 also traveled around the Moon. Two of its crew, Thomas Stafford and Eugene Cernan (above), were within a few miles (kilometers) of the surface in the lunar module, while the third astronaut, John Young, orbited the Moon.

The Apollo space suit

CONDITIONS ON THE MOON'S SURFACE do not support human life. The Apollo space suit provided each astronaut with everything necessary to survive the Moon's environment.

Liquid-cooled garment worn under the suit

An outer helmet with gold visor

A bubble helmet

Link to oxygen and life-support system worn as a backpack

Suit made of strong fibers, metals, and plastics

Gloves with molded fingertips

Outlet for transferring urine

A device for collecting urine

Lunar overshoe

Shoe with snap fastenings

Functions of the suit

The suit guarded the astronaut against micrometeoroids, tiny dust particles speeding through space. It controlled the astronaut's temperature by circulating cool water in an undergarment, and it protected the body against the lack of air pressure on the Moon.

TESTING AND BUILDING A ROCKET

IN MAY 1961, WHEN PRESIDENT KENNEDY PROMISED THAT the US would send a man to the Moon, there was no spacecraft capable of the task. So engineers and scientists set to work immediately to develop a suitable space vehicle. The Apollo craft was designed to carry the men to the Moon and bring them back to Earth again, and the Saturn V was created to launch them on their way. The various parts of Saturn V and Apollo were built and tested separately and then brought together at a specially constructed site at Cape Canaveral in Florida. The area known as Complex 39 included a giant building called the Vehicle Assembly Building (VAB) where the rocket was put together.

Rocket scientist
Wernher von Braun was the director of the team that developed the Saturn V rocket for the Moon. In 1968, when the rocket for Apollo 11 was under construction, 26,500 men and women were working at Cape Canaveral, Florida.

The Saturn V

MOST OF THE SATURN V rocket is filled with fuel. The Apollo 11 craft occupied a small part of the rocket.

Launch escape tower

Command module (*Columbia*)

Saturn V's cargo
The Apollo 11 takes up only the top end of Saturn V. Apollo 11 is made up of three parts, the command module *Columbia* the service module, and the lunar module *Eagle*.

Service module

Lunar module (*Eagle*)

The crew entered the spacecraft through the white room, 400 ft (122 m) above the ground.

The instrument unit was used for control and communication between Saturn V and Apollo.

The third stage moved Apollo into Earth orbit and then pointed it toward the Moon.

The Vehicle Assembly Building

A huge crane lifted the Apollo craft into position.

Super Guppy
The "Super Guppy" carried spacecraft parts to the VAB. It was one of two specially adapted planes with enlarged upper decks. The whole front section of the planes opened for loading and unloading.

The launch site

The rocket left the VAB two months before liftoff. The Saturn V moved through the giant doors and into the open air to start its journey into space. It was carried to launch pad 39A, 3.5 miles (5.6 km) away, by a crawler. A new launch site for the missions had been built on 140,000 acres (566,600 hectares) of land.

Nine swing arms connected the launch tower to the various levels of the Apollo and Saturn V craft.

The crawler could raise or lower one of its corners to keep the rocket level.

The five engines of the first stage extended into the 45 ft² (14m²) hole of the mobile launcher platform. At launch the engine's flames went into a flame trench.

CRAWLING ALONG
The crawler moved on eight tank-link tracks, each one 41 ft (12.5 m) long. It carried the Saturn V and its mobile launcher, which together weigh 6,600 tons (6,000 tonnes) at 1 mph (1.6 kph).

THE FINAL CHECKS

Inside the VAB, the parts were placed on top of each other and then checked and rechecked many times to see if the rocket worked when it was all together. The complete checklist filled more than 30,000 pages. Television cameras were also used to monitor what was happening. Once the final test sequence – a mock countdown that took the rocket to within 14 seconds of liftoff – was successfully completed, the craft was approved for launch.

The second stage, and below it the first stage, lifted the rocket off the ground and into space.

The first Saturn V rocket had been launched in 1967, this was the sixth Saturn V rocket.

The driver in the operator's cab was one of a 15-person crew who maneuvered the crawler.

BUILDING THE PARTS

The Saturn V is made up of three stages, each with a different role to perform during the rocket's launch and short flight. These stages and the Apollo craft were constructed by different engineering firms at locations across the US. Once the parts were completed and tested they were brought to the VAB for assembly.

Once complete the Saturn V rocket was as tall as a 24-floor building. It was 363 ft (111 m) high and powerful enough to lift the 50-ton (45-tonnes) Apollo craft off the ground.

Each of the three rocket stages had engines, a fuel tank, and an oxygen tank needed to burn the fuel.

The tanks fed kerosene fuel and liquid oxygen to an F-1 engine, during tests in California.

A ramp covered by a constant stream of water kept the flames down.

MOST POWERFUL ENGINES

Each of the rocket's stages had engines. The most powerful were those built for the first stage, which had to lift the rocket and its Apollo cargo off the launch pad. The five F-1 engines would only burn for two and a half minutes but in that time they would generate 7,600,000 lb (3,450,000 kg) of thrust to lift the 2,900-ton (2,630-tonne) Saturn V. They were the most powerful engines ever built.

GAS GUZZLERS
The engines consumed 16.5 tons (15 tonnes) of fuel per second at launch.

Blast Off!

A RMSTRONG, ALDRIN, AND COLLINS SAT CALMLY on top of the largest rocket in the world. Sealed inside the Saturn V, the astronauts carefully ran through their final checklist. The launch countdown was nearly complete. Thirty seconds to liftoff and everything was fine; the astronauts reported feeling good. Their incredible journey to the Moon was about to begin.

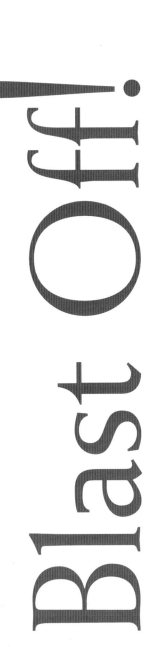

In an emergency, the escape tower would carry the astronauts in the command module, clear of the launch site.

The crew were located in the command module at the top of the rocket.

THE DAY OF LIFTOFF

THE CREW OF APOLLO 11 HAD AN EARLY CALL on July 16, 1969. They were awakened at 4:15 a.m., and after a brief medical examination they sat down for breakfast. Today's menu was special. It was steak, eggs, toast, orange juice, and coffee. It would be their last meal for a while. In four hours' time they would be sitting inside the Apollo command module (*Columbia*) at the top of the Saturn V rocket waiting to blast off to the Moon. The five-hour task of filling the rocket with fuel was almost complete. Now the three men, Neil Armstrong, commander, Edwin Aldrin, lunar module pilot, and Michael Collins, command module pilot, had to put on their space suits and travel to the launch pad.

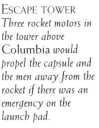

ESCAPE TOWER
Three rocket motors in the tower above Columbia *would propel the capsule and the men away from the rocket if there was an emergency on the launch pad.*

Columbia was named after the Italian explorer Christopher Columbus.

REST DAY
On Tuesday, July 15, the day before the launch, the crew had a rest day. This gave them the chance to relax before the demanding work of the next ten days. In the evening, the astronauts dined with their standby crews and their trainer.

SUITING UP
5:30 a.m. When the men arrived in the suiting-up room, everything was ready. The lead suit technician Joe Schmitt had been checking their clothes for the past two hours. Armstrong packed a snack into his suit before he dressed.

WALKING OUT
6:26 a.m. The men walked out from the living quarters to the transfer van to be taken to the launch pad. They carried their life-support systems as they walked. Their suits and the van bore the mission badge, showing an American eagle landing on the Moon. The lunar module was named *Eagle*.

INTO THE ROCKET
6:52 a.m. The men left the surface of Earth when they stepped into the elevator for the 32-second ride to the top of Saturn V. Waiting for them was the "close out" team. They helped the men into their seats, hooked up their suit hoses, and checked that *Columbia* was ready.

LIFTOFF

8:32 a.m.

The launch was on schedule and all the checks went smoothly. Once the firing command button was pressed at launch control, the automatic launch sequence began. Three minutes, ten seconds later, Apollo 11 started its 251,000-mile (403,913-km) journey to the Moon.

Nine seconds before launch the engines ignited and water gushed through the flame pit.

Into space

THE SATURN V rocket carried Apollo 11 into space to start its journey to the Moon.

Liftoff for the Moon
The liftoff was perfect and everything went as expected. The first few seconds of flight were noisy and jerky, but they were followed by a smooth ride through Earth's atmosphere. Only 11 minutes after liftoff, Apollo orbited Earth at 18,000 mph (29,000 kph).

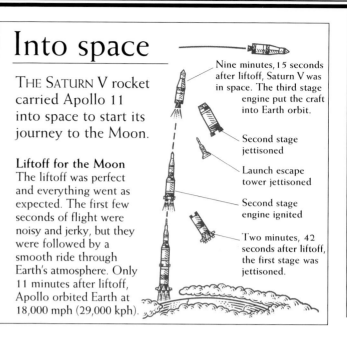

Nine minutes, 15 seconds after liftoff, Saturn V was in space. The third stage engine put the craft into Earth orbit.

Second stage jettisoned

Launch escape tower jettisoned

Second stage engine ignited

Two minutes, 42 seconds after liftoff, the first stage was jettisoned.

SEALED INSIDE
The arm swung back 43 minutes before launch.

The close out team worked in an area called "the White Room."

WAITING TO BOARD
Collins, and in front of him, Aldrin, waited as Armstrong climbed into Columbia.

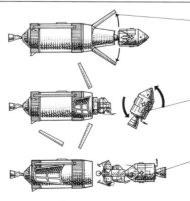

ONE MILLION SPECTATORS

The day was hot and sunny with a thin cloud layer, the best weather for a launch. One million people traveled to Florida to watch the beginning of the Apollo 11 journey. Though they couldn't see the astronauts, the astronauts could see the crowds from the top of the launch tower.

ON THE SHORE
Crowds stood along the shore in Florida to watch the Saturn V rocket on the launch pad.

FACT file

- Apollo began its journey not aimed at the Moon, but at where the Moon would be in three days' time.

- Five hours, 15 minutes, after launch, the astronauts ate their first meal in space: beef, potatoes, and grape juice.

- Fourteen hours after liftoff, the crew fastened covers over *Columbia's* windows and settled down to sleep.

- As the Apollo craft traveled, it rotated slowly, so that one side would not face the Sun constantly and overheat.

Heading for the Moon

THE APOLLO CRAFT separated from the final stage of the Saturn V rocket and prepared for the Moon.

Apollo docking
The Apollo craft and the third stage of the Saturn V rocket orbited Earth, and then moved onto a path for the Moon. After turning and docking maneuvers, the astronauts discarded the Saturn V rocket.

The combined command and service module separated from the rocket 3 hours and 15 minutes after liftoff.

The module turned around. Panels protecting the lunar module were discarded.

The command module docked with the lunar module and moved away from the third stage of the rocket.

MISSION CONTROL

ARMSTRONG, ALDRIN, AND COLLINS were on their way to the Moon. Though there were only three men in the craft, a team of people back on Earth felt that they were traveling with them. Every movement made by the craft or men was followed inside the mission operations control room in Houston, Texas. The engineers and technicians in this room kept in touch with the astronauts through sea-, air-, and land-based tracking stations. They made sure everything went according to plan and were ready for any emergency.

Flight director
The officer in charge of the control room and its work was the flight director. If any problems arose, the flight director was the person to make the final decision, after consulting the team members. Gene Kranz (above) was flight director for the landing.

Capsule communicator
The link between the control room and Apollo 11 was the capsule communicator, usually called "capcom." He handled all communication between Earth and the spacecraft. Capcom for the landing on the Moon was Charles Duke (above).

The front row of consoles was called "the trench."

Screens displayed the progress of the mission

Experiments officer

Capcom

Flight director

Operations and procedures officer

Control Room Team

EACH CONTROL ROOM TEAM was made up of smaller teams led by a controller or officer. They sat and worked together in the control room.

Flight dynamics officer
This officer is responsible for planning spacecraft maneuvers and monitoring the path taken by Apollo 11.

Experiments officer
When the astronauts are on the surface, this officer relays information between them and scientists on Earth.

Flight surgeon
The flight surgeon monitors the health of the crew during the course of the flight.

Flight activities officer
This officer plans the crew's tasks, and makes sure they follow their checklists and schedules during the flight.

Network controller
This controller coordinates the worldwide network of communication links.

Retrofire officer
If something goes wrong on a mission, the retrofire officer advises when to return home.

CONTROL ROOM

Four teams took turns working around the clock at mission control. Once a team was in position, the doors were locked so that they couldn't be disturbed. Each member of the team monitored a part of the mission. This might mean studying the route of the Apollo 11, guiding its descent to the Moon, or checking the health of the crew. The teams sat at computer consoles displaying up-to-date information on their area of responsibility.

GLOBAL LINK
Three large antennae based in Australia, Spain, and California, were the core of the tracking system. The antenna at Honeysuckle Creek, near Canberra, Australia, was 85ft (26 m) in diameter.

On track for the Moon

APOLLO 11'S MISSION started in Florida. The Saturn V rocket lifted the craft into orbit around Earth and then on course for the Moon.

Mid-course correction

Eagle separated.

Into Moon orbit
After orbiting Earth, they moved on course for the Moon, and Saturn V's job was over. When Apollo 11 and its crew reached the Moon, they went into orbit around it. Then *Eagle* separated and approached the Moon ready to land.

Columbia docked with *Eagle*.

Aircraft with antennae flew to areas without land or sea stations.

The tracking ship Vanguard *was positioned in the Atlantic Ocean.*

KEEPING TRACK
A network of ground, ship, and air tracking stations called the Manned Spaceflight Network (MSFN) allowed mission control to know where Apollo was at anytime. It also relayed messages between capcom and the astronauts.

COMMUNICATING
Four tracking ships not only helped to locate Apollo11 but also worked as part of the communication system. They relayed information from the craft and the men.

Flight dynamics officer

Network controller

Steve Bales, guidance officer

Gene Kranz, flight director

SPECIAL GUESTS
Off-duty officers, astronauts, family, and invited guests watched from behind glass.

DECISION TO LAND
As Armstrong and Aldrin moved closer to the Moon, an alarm sounded. In the control room a flashing light let the ground team know that *Eagle*'s computer had too many jobs to do at once. Flight director Gene Kranz consulted guidance officer Steve Bales. Could the landing go ahead? The message "We're go" was passed to Armstrong.

HOMEWARD BOUND

THE APOLLO 11 astronauts heard the engines roar and knew they were on their way home. The engines burned (fired) for a short time to push the craft out of the Moon's orbit and on its way back to Earth. *Eagle*, which had lifted Armstrong and Aldrin from the lunar surface, had been jettisoned. Just two parts of the *Apollo* craft, the command and service modules, would make the journey back. The men received congratulations from the ground crew and settled down for a well-earned sleep. They rested for 10 hours. A major part of their mission was now over, but the hazardous reentry into Earth's atmosphere, followed by the splashdown in the Pacific Ocean, still lay ahead.

RADIO SILENCE
Radio links with the ground ceased for about 15 minutes as they traveled through the upper atmosphere.

Friction, caused by the craft rushing through the air, heated the outside of the capsule.

HEAT SHIELD
The walls of the capsule were built like a multilayered sandwich. The outer heat shield was designed to burn off.

HEATING UP
Inside the craft, the temperature remained a constant 80°F (27°C). Temperatures on the base of the craft reached 5,000°F (2,760°C).

Back to Earth

THE ASTRONAUTS STARTED their journey home in the combined command and service modules.

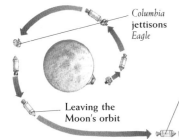

Columbia jettisons *Eagle*

Leaving the Moon's orbit

RETURN TRIP
The journey home began when Apollo 11 left Moon orbit on July 22, 1969. As the module reentered Earth's atmosphere it was traveling at almost 25,000 mph (40,300 kph).

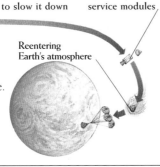

Correction to *Columbia*'s course to slow it down

Separation of command and service modules

Reentering Earth's atmosphere

Preparing for Earth's atmosphere
The service module was jettisoned before it reached Earth's atmosphere. *Columbia* was traveling nose first until thrusters were used to turn it around so that the blunt end was pointing toward Earth. The Earth's atmosphere slowed the craft.

THROUGH EARTH'S ATMOSPHERE
As they headed toward Earth, Armstrong, Aldrin, and Collins showed the world on a live television broadcast the Moon rocks they had collected. Close to Earth, they jettisoned the service module. *Columbia* with its cargo of men and rocks would be the only part of Apollo 11 to return to Earth. The craft sped through the atmosphere, burning up on the outside. Inside, Armstrong used small thrusters to control the direction of the craft.

SLOWING DOWN

At 20,000 ft (6,000 m) above the ground, and with Columbia traveling at 325 mph (525 kph), the parachute landing system started.

The cone tip of Columbia was cast off and two parachutes were used to help slow down the craft.

PARACHUTE FALL

The location for splashdown was chosen before the craft entered the atmosphere. There were two tropical storms near the recovery area that had to be avoided. The module was directed toward good weather where the visibility was 10 miles (16 km). Once through the upper atmosphere, the module's parachutes slowed the craft in its last stage of descent.

INTO THE OCEAN
At 10,000 ft (3,000 m) the three main parachutes opened slowing the module to 20 mph (32 kph). Columbia *splashed down exactly 195 hours and 18 minutes after leaving Earth.*

The blunt side was designed to slow down the craft on its return to Earth.

The recovery ship Hornet *took the astronauts and their module to Hawaii, from where they flew to Houston, Texas.*

The Mobile Quarantine Facility
Richard Nixon, President of the US, was on board *Hornet* waiting to welcome the three astronauts home. After a shower and shave, they appeared at the window and joined in prayers of thanksgiving for their safe return. The astronauts stayed in quarantine for two weeks in the Lunar Receiving Laboratory in Houston, where they were examined by doctors.

The helicopter Recovery 1 flew the astronauts the short distance from the dinghy to the lower deck of Hornet.

SPLASHDOWN

Columbia splashed down into the Pacific Ocean. It floated upside down, until Collins activated three flotation bags stowed in the module's nose. Within five minutes, the craft was upright. Two rescue teams in their dinghies and frogmen in the water moved toward the module. The rescue ship *Hornet* was close by, ready to take the astronauts home.

The Mobile Quarantine Facility (MQF) was home to the astronauts for three and a half days.

The frogmen placed a flotation collar around the module to stop it from sinking.

A frogman cleaned the hatch of the module with disinfectant to kill any Moon germs.

The recovery dinghies were disinfected and then sunk.

BACK ON EARTH
The men had their first experience for several days of walking in Earth's gravity, as they moved from the helicopter to the MQF.

CLIMBING OUT

A frogman opened the door of the module and passed special overalls to the three men. The astronauts put these on to protect others from the Moon dust on their clothes. Once in the dinghy, Armstrong, Collins, and Aldrin were hoisted aboard the helicopter.

Welcome home
Once they were out of quarantine, the three astronauts could relax and celebrate with their families and people around the world. Vast numbers of people turned out to see them in the 23 countries they visited in a 38-day tour. In New York City they were welcomed with a ticker-tape (paper ribbon) parade.

Later Missions

WITHIN MONTHS OF THE FIRST MEN RETURNING safely to Earth, a second crew was heading toward the Moon and others were preparing to go. In all, 12 men landed on the Moon – two more astronauts had to abandon their plans and return disappointed. Since 1972, exploration has been restricted to robotic craft, but today a new generation is preparing to return to the Moon.

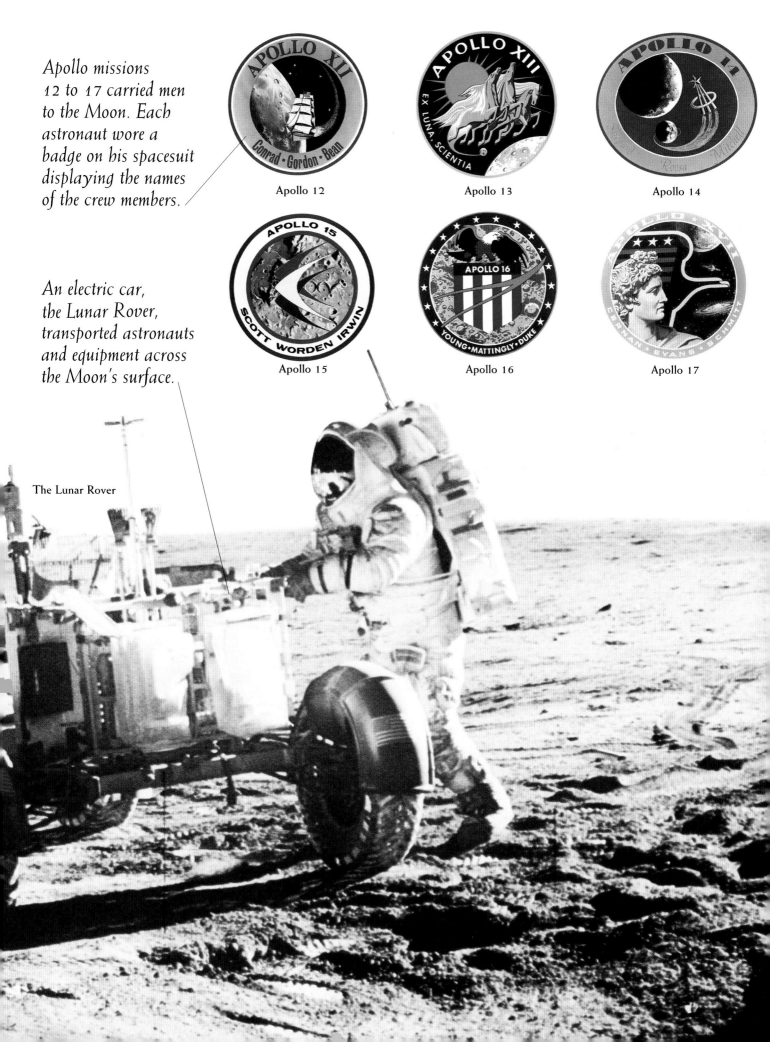

Apollo missions 12 to 17 carried men to the Moon. Each astronaut wore a badge on his spacesuit displaying the names of the crew members.

Apollo 12

Apollo 13

Apollo 14

An electric car, the Lunar Rover, transported astronauts and equipment across the Moon's surface.

Apollo 15

Apollo 16

Apollo 17

The Lunar Rover

Laser reflector experiment
The astronauts set up experiments such as this laser ranging retro reflector. Its upper mirrored surface reflected a laser beam back to Earth to provide information on the Moon's orbit.

Seismometer equipment
Other experiments were part of a package. These consisted of a number of experiments linked to a central transmitter. This seismometer collected data on moonquakes.

EXPLORING THE MOON

FIVE MORE APOLLO MISSIONS CARRIED astronauts to the Moon's surface. These later missions could concentrate on making a scientific investigation of the lunar landscape. The astronauts worked in four-hour shifts, collecting samples and setting up experiments. Although the men only stayed for a few days at a time, the experiments operated for several years. The first crews carried their tools or pulled them along on a handcart. But in the later missions they used a Rover for getting around. This unique lunar car gave them the freedom to travel away from their landing site. By the time the last mission left the Moon, its different types of landscape: mare, lowlands, highlands, and craters had all been explored.

Rock collecting

THE ASTRONAUTS' SPACE SUITS restricted their movements. The gloves were thick and clumsy, and the astronauts were unable to bend in their suits. Special tools were designed to make it possible to collect rocks without bending. These tools had to be transported from site to site along with boxes of rock samples. Though they weren't heavy in the Moon's gravity, they were bulky to carry around.

A tool rack fitted into the frame of the rickshaw.

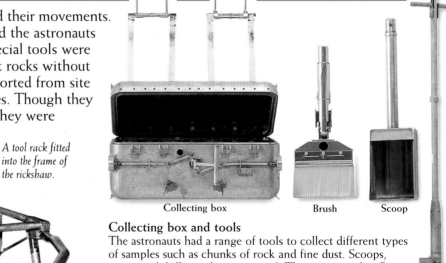

Collecting box   Brush   Scoop

Collecting box and tools
The astronauts had a range of tools to collect different types of samples such as chunks of rock and fine dust. Scoops, tongs, and drilling tubes were used. The astronauts briefly described the sample and the site it came from, put it in a bag and then into a storage box.

Metal fingers grasped the rock.   Tongs

The air-pumped tires became stuck in deep Moon dust and the rickshaw had to be carried.

The rickshaw
The Apollo 14 astronauts had a Modularized Equipment Transporter for carrying their tools, cameras, and samples. This handcart, usually called a "rickshaw," was pulled along by the astronauts and allowed them to collect a greater number of samples.

The Rover

THE ROVER WAS CARRIED to the Moon underneath the lunar module. It was lowered for use.

Unfolding the Rover
The Rover was complete but folded for the journey. Once on the Moon, an astronaut pulled two cords to lower it. Each end of the vehicle unfolded and the wheels moved out into position.

THE FINAL MISSION
The last manned mission to the Moon, Apollo 17, began on December 7, 1972. It was the first manned launch at night. Two of the crew, Eugene Cernan and Harrison Schmitt, spent the longest time on the lunar surface – 22 hours. Schmitt, a geologist, was the only scientist to land on the Moon.

A plaque like this one, was fixed to the descent stage of Challenger, which was left behind on the Moon.

The plaque marked the end of human exploration of the Moon.

HERE MAN COMPLETED HIS FIRST EXPLORATIONS OF THE MOON DECEMBER 1972, A.D. MAY THE SPIRIT OF PEACE IN WHICH WE CAME BE REFLECTED IN THE LIVES OF ALL MANKIND

A MESSAGE
The Apollo 17 lunar module, named *Challenger*, landed near the edge of the Mare Serenitatis. When the astronauts blasted off on December 14, 1972, they left behind a plaque.

Antenna

Television camera

Antenna for communication

Hand control for driving

COMMUNICATION
The astronauts could talk to each other as they worked, through a communication antenna in their backpack.

The wheels were made of wire mesh and each contained its own motor.

Tools were fitted in a rack at the back of the Rover. Rock samples were placed in front of the rack and under the seats.

MOON ROVING
A Lunar Roving Vehicle, usually called the "Rover," was used on Apollos 15, 16, and 17. It was a lightweight car powered by two batteries and had a top speed of 11 mph (18.6 kph). The astronauts used it to travel up to 6 miles (9.6 km) from their landing site. They could not travel any farther because if it broke down, it would be too far to walk back.

The Rover was built mainly from aluminum, a lightweight metal that helped to keep the weight down.

EYEWITNESS
"Houston, we've had a problem here."
John Swigert to mission control, April 13, 1970

DESPERATE MEASURES
Apollo 13 traveled around the Moon. It used the lunar module's engine to put the craft on a course back toward Earth.

LIFE-SUPPORT SYSTEM
The lunar module was designed to support two men for two days on the Moon It was now needed to support three men for at least six days.

DISASTER STRIKES!

JAMES LOVELL, JOHN SWIGERT, AND FRED Haise were approaching the Moon on the Apollo 13 mission. They were looking forward to exploring its surface. The men had just completed a television broadcast when they were interrupted by a sharp bang. A warning light flashed on, and the Apollo craft shuddered. Something was wrong. The men discovered that there had been an explosion in the service module that provided the crew with vital power and life-support systems. Things couldn't have been worse. They were 200,000 miles (322,000 km) from Earth heading for the Moon without the power to turn around.

There was an explosion in the service module.

Oxygen tank number 1 was damaged, and its contents escaped into space.

A course correction aimed Apollo 13 at Earth.

The service module

The lunar module

The astronauts moved into the lunar module, which had its own supply of oxygen, water, and power.

The command module

A whole panel of the service module was blown off.

Oxygen tank number 2 blew up.

FIRE AND DEBRIS
Pieces of insulating foil were blown out into space. The flames stopped when all the oxygen had escaped.

Oxygen tanks
The number 2 oxygen tank had overheated and exploded. Its temperature should have been controlled, but the switches had become welded shut. The temperature of the tank should not have been higher than 80°F (27°C) but it soared to 1,000°F (538°C).

EXPLOSION!
The crew reported the explosion to mission control. The warning lights told them they had lost their main source of electricity. They knew this meant the planned landing on the Moon would be abandoned, but disappointment quickly turned to thoughts of survival. Every effort from the astronauts and mission control was needed to get the men home.

BRING THEM HOME
Four teams at mission control, the black, gold, white, and maroon teams, worked in shifts around the clock to find the best way to bring Apollo 13 back home. They had decided to use the lunar module's engines to bring the astronauts back.

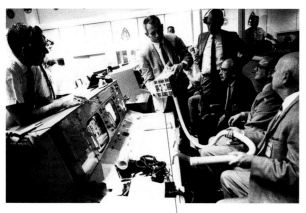

The ground team used only the items that could be found on Apollo 13, such as cardboard, tape, and plastic bags.

MORE PROBLEMS

Haise told mission control that the lunar module had enough oxygen and power to make the journey home, if they turned off everything that was not essential. But the lunar module was filling with the carbon dioxide that the crew were breathing out. Ground teams worked to build something to take the carbon dioxide out of the air.

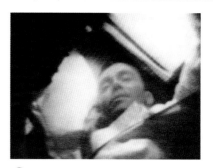

COLD AND DAMP

Conditions inside the lunar module were grim. The temperature dropped to 38°F (3°C). Water condensed on the walls, and the windows were covered with frost. The men found it hard to sleep. The food they ate was very cold, and altogether they lost 31.5 lbs (14 kg) in weight.

Haise watched the work.

The command module's air-cleaning equipment was adapted for the lunar module.

SAVING THEIR LIVES

After one and a half days, and before the carbon dioxide level became dangerous, the ground crew built a piece of equipment to clean the carbon dioxide from the air in the lunar module. Inside the command module, Lovell and Swigert were led step-by-step through the process to build the same piece of equipment. One hour later, they had finished, and another problem was solved.

A hose taken from a space suit

Swigert followed instructions from Earth.

Relief and disappointment
The astronauts were picked up from the Pacific Ocean by the recovery ship *Iwo Jima*. They were all hungry, tired, dehydrated, and cold. In the final hours before recovery they had used stimulants to keep them alert. The flight was a disappointment for Lovell; he had now traveled to the Moon twice without landing on it.

Apollo 13 made a course adjustment and headed for a lunar landing.

GETTING CLOSER
The lunar module that acted as a lifeboat for the three astronauts had done its job, now that they were close to Earth.

Apollo 13 started its journey from Earth on April 11, 1970.

The crew had their first look at the damage and photographed it.

THE FINAL HOUR
The astronauts moved from the lunar module to the command module for the journey through Earth's atmosphere.

A SAFE RETURN
The command module and its crew of three astronauts splashed down on April 17th. The mission was described as a successful failure because of the men's safe return.

NO MORE USE
About four hours before splashdown, the crew jettisoned the useless service module.

THE FINAL STAGE

The three astronauts traveled toward Earth in the lunar module and then moved into the command module for the final stage of the journey. They turned on its equipment; it was cold and wet but operated as normal. The wrecked service module and the lunar module were jettisoned now that their work was over.

Samples were put in this capsule and returned to Earth.

SCIENTIFIC INVESTIGATIONS

WHILE THE US WAS BUSY SENDING MEN TO the Moon, Soviet rockets were launching robotic probes to explore the lunar surface. Twenty-four Luna missions were sent between 1959 and 1976. Three brought back rocks to Earth, and two carried mobile scientific laboratories to work on the Moon's surface. In the 18 years following the final Luna mission, neither crewed nor robotic craft were sent to the Moon. Scientists continued to work on information and samples that had already been collected. Much of the Apollo rock was studied at the specially built Lunar Sample Building in Houston, Texas.

ROCK SAMPLES

Luna 16 was the first robotic probe to bring back rock from the Moon. The probe made a controlled landing on the Moon in September 1970. Luna 16's drill collected a sample from 14 in (35 cm) below the surface. The drill was in the lower part of the probe. The upper part of the probe had its own engine and fuel, and returned the sample to Earth.

Luna 20 returned to Earth during a snowstorm on February 25, 1972.

FURTHER SAMPLES

Luna 20 brought the second sample back to Earth in February 1972. The sample of soil from beneath the surface of the Moon was well protected on its journey. The outside of the returning capsule screened the rock from the high temperatures of the Earth's upper atmosphere. A parachute slowed the probe's fall, and a radio signal indicated its location.

Equipment to turn the antenna to point toward Earth for receiving and sending information

Antenna

Scientific instruments sealed inside the instrument bay

Radiator to keep Lunokhod 1 cool

X-ray telescope

Television camera

Soil analysis equipment

ROBOT EXPLORER

Lunokhod 1 was the first of two robotic craft to move around on the lunar surface and work at different sites. It landed in the Mare Imbrium in November 1970. During the next ten months it moved over 6.5 miles (10.45 km) of the lunar surface. Operators on Earth controlled its movements. It returned more than 20,000 pictures to Earth and tested the soil at 500 points. An upgraded Lunokhod arrived on the Moon to start work in 1973. It worked for less than five months but traveled farther, 23 miles (37 km).

Moon rocks

THE APOLLO ASTRONAUTS collected 2,000 samples of rock, pebbles, sand, dust, and core material. The samples were studied around the world.

Breccia rocks

Many of the rocks collected by John Young and Charles Duke on the Apollo 16 mission were breccias from the rugged highlands. These rocks were produced when space rocks crashed into the Moon, melting and pushing together the rock and soil on the Moon's surface.

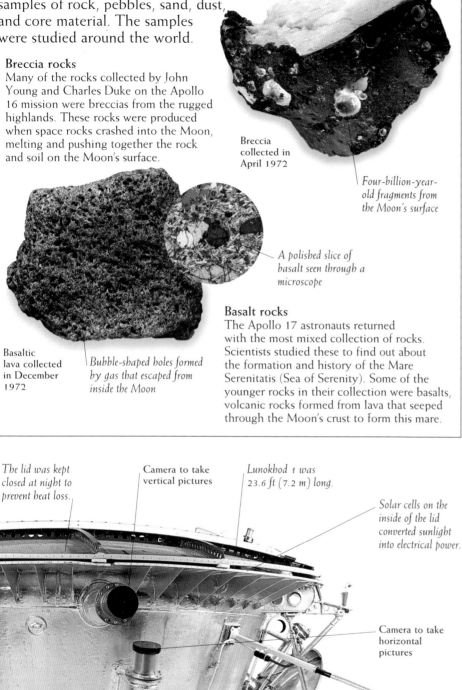

Breccia collected in April 1972

Four-billion-year-old fragments from the Moon's surface

A polished slice of basalt seen through a microscope

Basaltic lava collected in December 1972

Bubble-shaped holes formed by gas that escaped from inside the Moon

Basalt rocks

The Apollo 17 astronauts returned with the most mixed collection of rocks. Scientists studied these to find out about the formation and history of the Mare Serenitatis (Sea of Serenity). Some of the younger rocks in their collection were basalts, volcanic rocks formed from lava that seeped through the Moon's crust to form this mare.

The lid was kept closed at night to prevent heat loss.

Camera to take vertical pictures

Lunokhod 1 was 23.6 ft (7.2 m) long.

Solar cells on the inside of the lid converted sunlight into electrical power.

Camera to take horizontal pictures

The eight wheels had titanium bars to grip the lunar surface.

Lunokhod 1

FACT file

- Between 1959 and 1998 more than 60 crewed and robotic spacecraft successfully traveled to the Moon.
- Three new minerals were discovered on the lunar surface; one was named armalcolite in honor of Armstrong, Aldrin, and Collins.
- The Apollo astronauts set up over 50 experiments on six sites on the Moon.
- Clementine orbited the Moon 351 times and returned more than 1,800,000 images of the lunar surface to Earth.

Clementine's survey

When the space probe Clementine moved into orbit around the Moon in February 1994, it was the first US craft to investigate the Moon since Apollo 17 had more than 20 years earlier. Clementine made a photographic survey of 99 percent of the Moon's surface, including the polar regions, during the following three months.

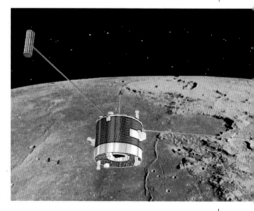

Lunar Prospector

Instruments aboard the Prospector probe started work on January 12, 1998, as the craft orbited 62 miles (100 km) above the lunar surface. Data received from one of the instruments suggested that water ice is mixed with surface soil in the polar regions, particularly around the North Pole. If the findings are correct, parts of the Moon may not be dry and lifeless after all.

MOON DATA

THE MOON IS AN ENORMOUS ball of rock that shines in our sky by reflected sunlight. Our present knowledge of it is based on what we see through telescopes on Earth and in space, and on information collected by the Apollo missions and scores of other spacecraft that have investigated the Moon. We know not only what the Moon is like today, but also how it was formed and what it was like in the past.

THE NEAR SIDE
The same side of the Moon, called its near side, always faces Earth. Dark and light areas on the surface are easily visible from Earth. Early observers mistook the dark regions as seas and called them "maria," the Latin word for seas.

The dark, low-lying maria (singular mare) are huge craters filled with lava.

Mare Tranquillitatis is one of the largest maria and was the landing site for Apollo 11.

Copernicus is a young, bright crater.

MARE IMBRIUM
MARE SERENITATIS
OCEANUS PROCELLARUM
Copernicus
MARE TRANQUILLITATIS
MARE CRISIUM
MARE FECUNDITATIS
Alphonsus
Tycho

LANDING SITES
17 Luna missions 17, 21
11 Apollo missions 11, 12, 14, 15, 16, 17

NEAR SIDE

The Moon is covered with craters, bowl-shaped hollows in its surface that formed when space rocks crashed into it.

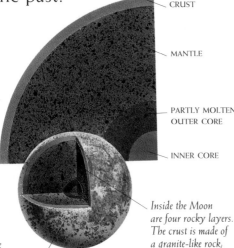

CRUST
MANTLE
PARTLY MOLTEN OUTER CORE
INNER CORE

Inside the Moon are four rocky layers. The crust is made of a granite-like rock; the inner core may be made of iron.

Surface rock and dust cover the crust.

The Moon's structure
The Moon is a sphere of rock about a quarter of the size of Earth. It is a dry world without atmosphere, life, or geological activity. It is Earth's only Moon and accompanies our planet as it orbits the Sun.

Facts and Figures

DIAMETER	2,158 MILES (3,476 KM)
AVERAGE DISTANCE FROM EARTH	239,000 MILES (384,400 KM)
ORBIT AROUND EARTH	27.3 DAYS
ORBITAL SPEED	0.6 MILES/SECOND (1.02 KM/SECOND)
ONE SPIN ON ITS AXIS	27.3 DAYS
CYCLE OF PHASES	29.5 DAYS
TEMPERATURE	-247°F TO 221°F (-155°C TO 105°C)
GRAVITY (EARTH = 1)	0.16
MASS (EARTH = 1)	0.012

THE MOON'S PAST
Most scientists believe the Moon was formed from Earth about 4.5 billion years ago. The young Moon's surface became covered in craters and lava.

Formation of the Moon
A rock about the size of Mars crashed into the young earth, splashing molten rock into orbit around it. The material joined together to form a big, molten Moon.

As the Moon cooled, its rock started to solidify and a crust formed on its surface. Craters appeared when space rocks crashed into the crust.

About 3 billion years ago, molten rock started to ooze through the crust and created maria, seas of lava on part of the Moon's surface.

Today's Moon looks like the Moon of about 2 billion years ago. There have been no major changes, just some new craters.

4.5 BILLION YEARS AGO   3.8 BILLION YEARS AGO   2.8 BILLION YEARS AGO   TODAY

44

THE FAR SIDE

The Moon's far side is invisible from Earth. Only the Apollo astronauts who flew to the Moon have seen it. The rest of us can see it in photographs taken by spacecraft. Like the near side, it is covered with craters, but has fewer, smaller maria.

Mare Moscoviense is one of the few maria on the far side. Less lava broke through on this side, because the crust is much thicker.

This side would be a good location for a telescope to study space.

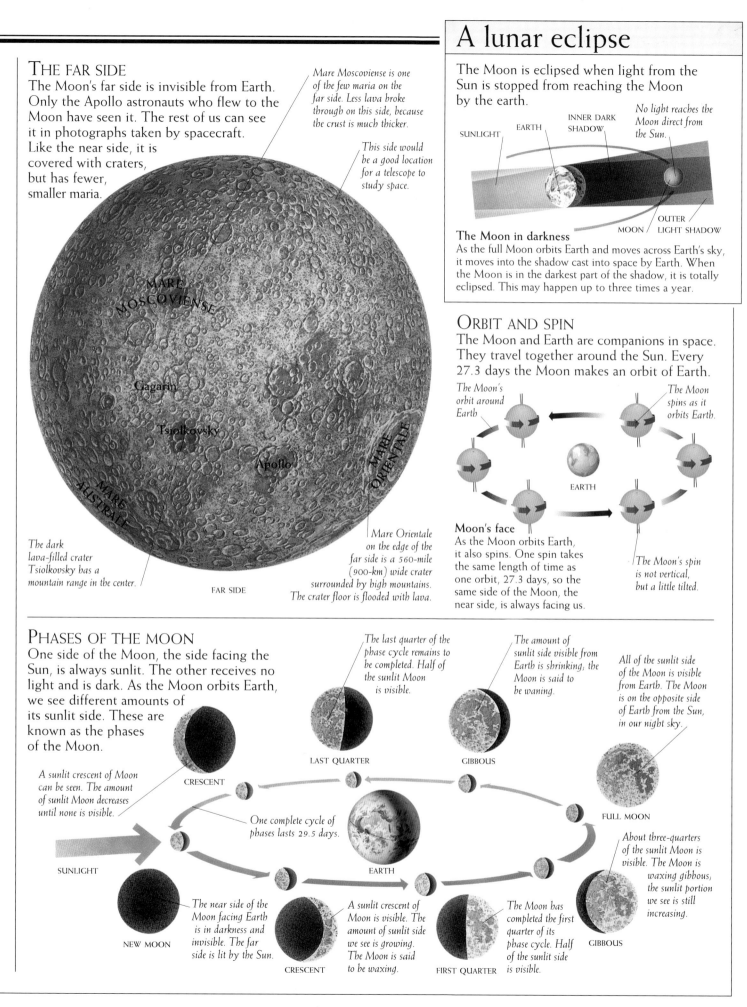

MARE MOSCOVIENSE

Gagarin

Tsiolkovsky

Apollo

MARE AUSTRALE

MARE ORIENTALE

The dark lava-filled crater Tsiolkovsky has a mountain range in the center.

Mare Orientale on the edge of the far side is a 560-mile (900-km) wide crater surrounded by high mountains. The crater floor is flooded with lava.

FAR SIDE

A lunar eclipse

The Moon is eclipsed when light from the Sun is stopped from reaching the Moon by the earth.

SUNLIGHT EARTH INNER DARK SHADOW *No light reaches the Moon direct from the Sun.*

MOON OUTER LIGHT SHADOW

The Moon in darkness
As the full Moon orbits Earth and moves across Earth's sky, it moves into the shadow cast into space by Earth. When the Moon is in the darkest part of the shadow, it is totally eclipsed. This may happen up to three times a year.

ORBIT AND SPIN

The Moon and Earth are companions in space. They travel together around the Sun. Every 27.3 days the Moon makes an orbit of Earth.

The Moon's orbit around Earth

The Moon spins as it orbits Earth.

EARTH

The Moon's spin is not vertical, but a little tilted.

Moon's face
As the Moon orbits Earth, it also spins. One spin takes the same length of time as one orbit, 27.3 days, so the same side of the Moon, the near side, is always facing us.

PHASES OF THE MOON

One side of the Moon, the side facing the Sun, is always sunlit. The other receives no light and is dark. As the Moon orbits Earth, we see different amounts of its sunlit side. These are known as the phases of the Moon.

The last quarter of the phase cycle remains to be completed. Half of the sunlit Moon is visible.

The amount of sunlit side visible from Earth is shrinking; the Moon is said to be waning.

All of the sunlit side of the Moon is visible from Earth. The Moon is on the opposite side of Earth from the Sun, in our night sky.

LAST QUARTER

GIBBOUS

FULL MOON

A sunlit crescent of Moon can be seen. The amount of sunlit Moon decreases until none is visible.

CRESCENT

One complete cycle of phases lasts 29.5 days.

EARTH

SUNLIGHT

The near side of the Moon facing Earth is in darkness and invisible. The far side is lit by the Sun.

NEW MOON

A sunlit crescent of Moon is visible. The amount of sunlit side we see is growing. The Moon is said to be waxing.

CRESCENT

The Moon has completed the first quarter of its phase cycle. Half of the sunlit side is visible.

FIRST QUARTER

About three-quarters of the sunlit Moon is visible. The Moon is waxing gibbous; the sunlit portion we see is still increasing.

GIBBOUS

MOON MISSIONS

LISTED BELOW ARE THE MOST successful missions to the Moon, including space missions that prepared the way for the first manned landing.

Sputnik 1
The first artificial satellite to orbit Earth. Launched by the Soviet Union on October 4, 1957. Successfully marked the start of the Space Age.

Sputnik 2
The first living creature to travel into space, Laika, a mongrel dog. Launched by the Soviet Union from Baikonur Cosmodrome, on November 3, 1957.

Luna 1
The first craft to leave Earth's gravity. The Soviet probe left Earth on January 2, 1959, and flew within 3,500 miles (5,630 km) of the Moon.

PIONEER 4

Pioneer 4
The first American probe to the Moon, launched two months after *Luna 1*. Three previous attempts had failed when the rockets couldn't achieve the necessary speed.

LUNA MISSIONS

Luna 2
The first craft to land on the Moon and the first to land on another celestial (heavenly) object. Crashed into the Moon on September 13, 1959.

Luna 3
Luna 3 was launched on the second anniversary of *Sputnik 1*. It flew around the Moon. On October 7, 1959, it radioed back to Earth the first pictures of the far side of the Moon.

Vostok 1
Soviet cosmonaut Yuri Gagarin traveled aboard *Vostok 1* and became the first human in space on April 12, 1961. He completed one orbit of Earth and landed safely, separate from his craft.

Mercury 3
Astronaut Alan Shepherd was the first American in space. His flight in the *Freedom 7* capsule lasted 15 minutes 22 seconds before splashdown on May 5, 1961.

Vostok 2
Gherman Titov was the second person in orbit and the first to spend more than 24 hours in space. The Soviet cosmonaut started his journey on August 6, 1961.

Mercury 6
John Glenn was the first American astronaut to fly in orbit around Earth. He was launched from Cape Canaveral on February 20, 1962. He made three orbits in *Friendship 7*.

Vostok 6
The first woman in space was Soviet cosmonaut Valentina Tereshkova. *Vostok 6* was launched on June 16, 1963, and spent 71 hours in space, orbiting Earth 38 times.

Solar panels provide the power for the cameras and for transmitting the pictures to Earth.

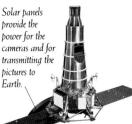

RANGER 7

Ranger 7
The seventh craft in the first American space program to explore the Moon. *Ranger 7* crashed into the Moon on July 31, 1964.

Voskhod 1
First three-man capsule into space, launched on October 12, 1964. Crew flew without space suits – no room for the Soviet cosmonauts to wear them. First live television transmission from space.

Ranger 8
Launched on February 17, 1965. Crash landed in the Mare Tranquillitatis, and transmitted over 7,000 photographs before impact on the Moon's surface.

Voskhod 2
Soviet cosmonaut Alexei Leonov made the first spacewalk on March 18, 1965. He was secured by a tether to his *Voskhod 2* capsule.

Ranger 9
The last in the American *Ranger* series. It transmitted nearly 6,000 photographs of the lunar surface before crash landing in the Alphonsus Crater.

Gemini 3
The first American two-man crew in space, launched on March 23, 1965. Gus Grissom and John Young were also the first American astronauts to maneuver a craft in space.

Gemini 4
Ed White was the first American astronaut to walk in space on June 3, 1965. He remained linked to his *Gemini* capsule by a tether during his 20-minute spacewalk.

Zond 3
A Soviet probe, launched on July 18, 1965, was destined for Mars; however, it flew past the Moon and sent back photographs of the Moon's far side.

Geminis 6 and 7
First American space rendezvous (link up) in December 1965. The two craft, each with two astronauts on board, met in orbit. Also the first time that there were four astronauts in space at the same time.

Luna 9
The first soft landing on the Moon. *Luna 9* sent the first television pictures from the lunar surface on February 3, 1966.

Gemini 8
The first space docking. Americans David Scott and Neil Armstrong flew into space on March 16, 1966, to dock with an unmanned *Agena* craft.

Luna 10
The first spacecraft to orbit the Moon. It achieved orbit on April 3, 1966, and started a study of the lunar surface.

SURVEYOR MISSIONS

Surveyor 1
First American probe to soft-land on the Moon. On June 2, 1966, it landed in the Oceanus Procellarum, tested the soil, and sent back over 11,000 photographs.

Lunar Orbiter 1
The first of five American probes to orbit and map the Moon. The *Orbiter* started work in August 1966 looking for lunar landing sites. On October 29, 1966, *Orbiter 1* was deliberately crashed into the surface to make room for *Orbiter 2*.

Lunar Orbiter 2
Orbiter 2 continued the work of *Orbiter 1* from November 1966. It located 13 possible landing sites before crashing in October 1967, to make room for *Orbiter 3*.

MEN ON THE MOON
The only humans to travel to the Moon were 26 US Apollo astronauts, all men. Of these, 12 walked on its surface, spending 80 hours exploring six different sites. The first to land was Neil Armstrong on July 20, 1969; the last was Eugene Cernan on December 14, 1972.

1969		1970
APOLLO 11 NEIL ARMSTRONG EDWIN ALDRIN		APOLLO 12 CHARLES CONRAD ALAN BEAN

Luna 13
A Soviet probe launched on December 21, 1966, that soft landed on the Moon. It transmitted pictures of the surface and used an arm digger to examine the composition of the lunar surface.

Lunar Orbiter 3
The third American *Orbiter* probe to orbit and photograph the Moon to help identify *Apollo* landing sites. It was launched on February 4, 1967.

Surveyor 3
An American probe soft landed on the Moon in April 1967. It tested the lunar soil and transmitted over 6,000 photographs of the surface. It remained in operation until early May 1967.

A camera with two lenses took photographs of the lunar surface.

LUNAR ORBITER

Lunar Orbiter 4
An American probe launched on May 4, 1967, that orbited and mapped the Moon. It took the first photographs of the Moon's south pole.

Lunar Orbiter 5
The last of the *Orbiter* series of probes designed to orbit and map the Moon. It transmitted photographs to Earth before crashing into the lunar surface on January 1, 1968.

Surveyor 5
An American probe soft landed in the Mare Tranquillitatis on September 10, 1967. It transmitted over 18,000 photographs and tested the lunar soil.

Surveyor 6
Launched on November 7, 1967, *Surveyor 6* made a soft landing on the Moon. It tested for a future liftoff from the Moon, rising 10 ft (3 m) above the ground.

Surveyor 7
The last *Surveyor* probe to the Moon. It landed near the crater Tycho in January 1968, tested the soil, and took photographs.

Zond 5
A Soviet spacecraft sent on September 14, 1968, to test equipment for a manned mission to the Moon. On board were turtles, worms, and flies. This was the first flight to circle the Moon and return to Earth.

Zond 6
The second Soviet craft launched to test equipment for a manned mission to the Moon. Sent on November 10, 1968, it circled the Moon and returned to Earth.

ZOND

Apollo 8
First manned flight of the *Saturn V* rocket on December 21, 1968 – the first manned craft to leave Earth's gravity. William Anders, James Lovell, and Frank Borman, were the first to orbit the Moon.

Apollo 9
First manned flight of spacecraft parts to be used to land on the Moon. In a ten-day trip, the crew docked with the Lunar Module in Earth orbit.

APOLLO 10

Apollo 10
A dress rehearsal for the lunar landing. American astronauts Tom Stafford and Eugene Cernan flew the Lunar Module close to the lunar surface on May 22, 1969.

Luna 15
Soviet probe *Luna 15* was launched for the Moon on July 13, 1969. It failed in its attempt to land a rover on the Moon and return it with a soil sample to Earth.

Apollo 11
The first men, American astronauts Neil Armstrong and Edwin Aldrin, walked on the Moon on July 20, 1969. Returned to Earth with Michael Collins.

Apollo 12
Second manned landing on the Moon. Landed on the Oceanus Procellarum on November 19, 1969. Walked to *Surveyor 3*, which had landed in 1967.

Apollo 13
An oxygen tank on *Apollo 13* exploded in flight in April 1970. The craft didn't land but returned to Earth safely.

Luna 16
First Soviet probe to collect Moon soil and return it to Earth. Landed at Mare Fecunditatis on September 20, 1970.

Luna 17
First wheeled vehicle on the Moon. *Lunokhod 1* explored Mare Imbrium on November 17, 1970. Tested the soil and sent back television pictures.

Apollo 14
Third manned landing on the Moon. Touched down on February 5, 1971, in the Fra Mauro hills. Used the handcart to carry tools and collected a large number of rocks.

Apollo 15
Fourth manned landing on the Moon and the first to use the Lunar Rover. Touched down on July 30, 1971, at Hadley Rille. Collected rocks.

Luna 20
Second Soviet mission to collect rock samples from the Moon. Brought back soil from Mare Crisium in February 1972.

Apollo 16
Fifth manned landing on the Moon on April 20, 1972. Landed in the lunar highlands at Cayley Formation. Used the second Lunar Rover to collect more rocks.

Apollo 17
Sixth and last manned mission to the Moon, landed on December 11, 1972, in the Littrow Valley. The Lunar Rover covered a greater area and collected a large number of rocks.

Luna 21
Carried the rover *Lunokhod 2* to the surface of the Moon. *Lunokhod 2* explored the surface for almost five months, until June 3, 1973.

Luna 23
Soviet probe launched to the Moon on October 28, 1974. Made a soft landing and returned soil samples to Earth.

LUNA

Luna 24
The last Soviet probe to bring back Moon soil samples to Earth. Samples were taken by drilling below the lunar surface.

Hiten
Probe launched to the Moon by Japan on January 24, 1990. *Hiten* carried a second probe, *Hagoromo*, making Japan only the third nation to put a craft into orbit around the Moon.

CLEMENTINE

Clementine
In February 1994, this American probe moved into orbit around the Moon. It started a program of mapping and investigating the lunar surface.

Lunar Prospector
American spacecraft *Lunar Prospector* went to the Moon in January 1998. Instruments investigating the Moon's surface detected signs of water ice near the north pole.

LUNAR PROSPECTOR

|1971| |1972|

APOLLO 14
ALAN SHEPARD
EDGAR MITCHELL

APOLLO 15
DAVID SCOTT
JAMES IRWIN

APOLLO 16
JOHN YOUNG
CHARLES DUKE

APOLLO 17
EUGENE CERNAN
HARRISON SCHMITT

Index

Acknowledgments

The publisher would like to thank: Anna Martin for design assistance, Chris Bernstein for the index, Robert Graham for research, and Lee Thompson for picture research.

Dorling Kindersley would like to thank the following institutions: Moscow Museum, NASA, Johnson Space Center and Headquarters, Washington, Polytechnic Museum, Moscow, Science Museum, London, US Space and Rocket Center, Alabama

The publisher would like to thank the following for their kind

permission to reproduce their photographs:

a=above; c=center, b=below; l=left; r=right; t=top;

BFI/Association des Amis de George Méliès Voyage to the Moon (Spadem 6 -7 tr; UPI/Corbis 26 cla, 26 tl, 31 cr; Corbis/Bettmann 24 cb, NASA 14 br, UPI/Corbis Bettmann 24 cl, 25 cr; John Frost Historical Newspapers/Evening Standard 11 crb: Genesis Space Photo Library/N.A.S.A 16 clb, 46 clb, 20 cl, 24 clb, 46 clb; Image Bank: Isy-Schwart 6 -7 cla; Peter

Inston/Inston Design International 43 tr; Courtesy of NASA : 8 crb, 12 -13, 14 cl, 15 clb, 15 cb, 17 cla, 17 crb, 17 bl, 18 crb, 18 -19 tc, 18 c, 19 tc, 19 clb, 20 br, 20 tr, 22 -23, 25 tl, 27 tl, 27 cra, 30 ca, 33 bl, 33 crb, 33 tr, 34 -35, 35 tc, 35 tl, 35 tr, 35 cla, 35 ca, 35 cra, 36 bl, 36 tl, 36 la, 37 . cra, 37 tr, 38 rb, 38 rb, 38 lb, 39 tl, 39 tr, 41 ca, 41 crb, 41 cr, 42 clb, 43 br, 46 c, 47 cl, 47 ca, 47 br; Natural History Museum, London 41 cra, 41 tl; Novosti (London): 9 cb, 10 tl, 11 tr, 14 tl, 15 tl, 17 tc, 40 tl, 40 lb, 47 clb, 47 clb, 47 cr; Oxford Scientific Films:

Stan Osilinski 6 -7; Science & Society Picture Library: 18 bl, 18 bc; Novosti/Science Photo Library: 9 cr; Small Space Photos: 30 tr; Sovfoto/Eastfoto 46 cla, 46 cla, 47 tr; Carole Stott 46 cr; Topham Picturepoint: 17 tr; TRH Pictures 16 bc

Jacket
Image Bank: Isy-Schwart back cra; N.A.S.A: front inside flap, front c, front cla, front cla, front bl, back inside flap, Novosti/Science Photo Library: back crb; US Space & Rocket Museum, Alabama: back bc